# NO MATTER WHAT PEOPLE SAY THIS BOOK IS NOT A DIARY.

# DUDE

## DIARY 2

WRITE STUFF

DRAW RANDOM THINGS

DESTROY IF NEEDED

WRITTEN &
DESIGNED BY
MICKEY
&
CHERYL
GILL

...and I helped.

FINE print
PUBLISHING

Fine Print Publishing Company
P.O. Box 916401
Longwood, Florida 32971-6401

Created in the U.S.A. & Printed in China
This book is printed on acid-free paper.

ISBN 978-1-89295153-3

2 3 5 7 9 10 8 6 4

**thedudebook.com**

MRAW

I wish I had a watch
that dispensed

- - - - - - - - - - - - - - -

- - - - - - - - - - - - - - -

- - - - - - - - - - -

Ben
Name of dude controlling
this Itiny

Last      thing
**that hit you?**
○ Ball
○ Bird poop
○ My brother

Don't know what it
means? Look it up man.

Measure
the
circum-
ference
of
your
head.

**Size of
your brain?**

- - - - - - - - - - - - - - - -

This is super scientific!

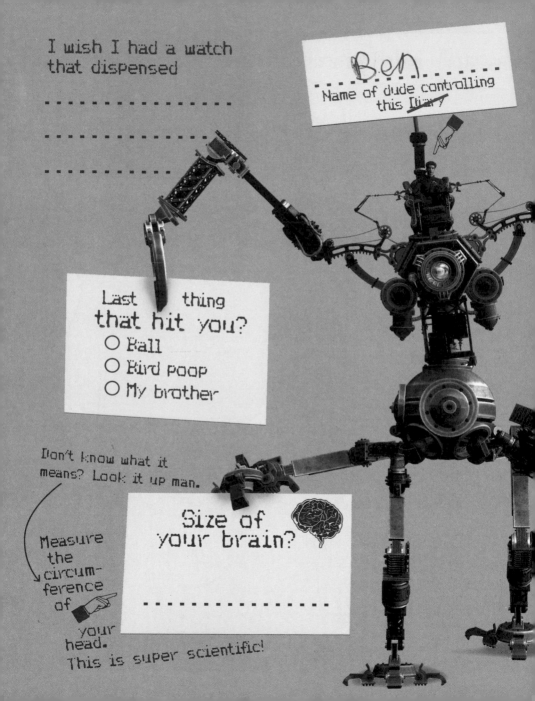

What's under your bed?
..a giant box

Favorite sci-fi or fantasy movie?
. . . . .

What do you have too much of?
① Earwax
○ Boogers
○ Hair
○ Nothing.
   I'm perfect.

What do you read?
○ Comics
⊘ Books
○ Magazines
○ Everything

Check: bloodsuckers that have attacked you.
○ Tick:   ○ Fleas
      ○ Mosquito
○ Other . . . . .

If you could have one bionic body part what would it be?

. . . . .

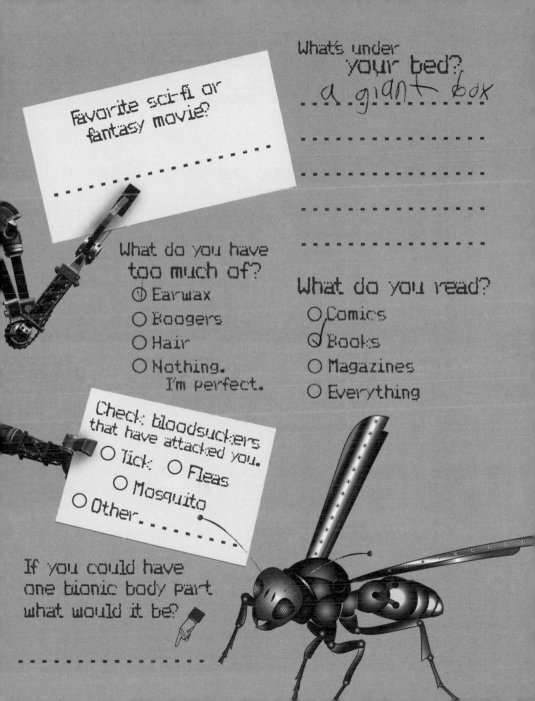

# IN THIS CORNER, IT'S

## ☆ THE CRUSHER!

# YOU'RE IN THE OTHER.

# DUDE, YOU NEED AN AWESOME PRO WRESTLER NAME.

ULTRA SUPERSPANKER

/I\

NEED SOME INSPIRATION? GO TO THEDUDEBOOK.COM/WRESTLER

Make a
# JUNK
drawer.
Empty out your
backpack or bedroom
drawers. Glue or tape
## down stuff.
Change, ticket stubs, wrappers,
lint, etc., etc. The weirder,
the better.

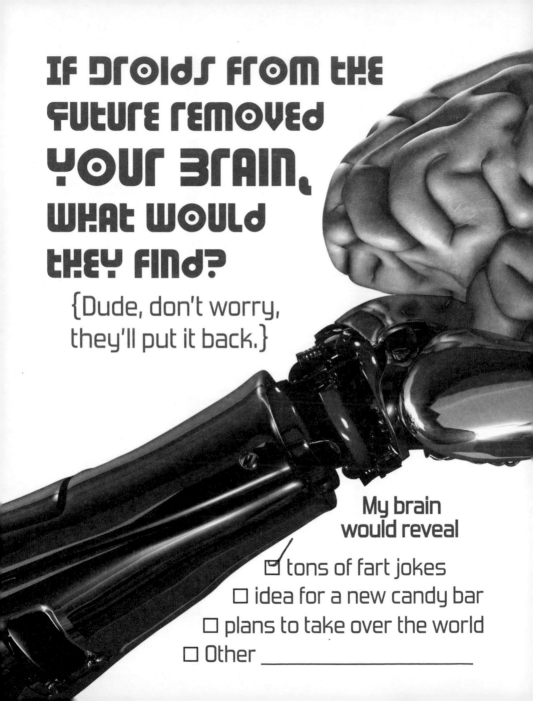

IF DROIDS FROM THE FUTURE REMOVED YOUR BRAIN, WHAT WOULD THEY FIND?

{Dude, don't worry, they'll put it back.}

My brain would reveal

☑ tons of fart jokes
☐ idea for a new candy bar
☐ plans to take over the world
☐ Other _____

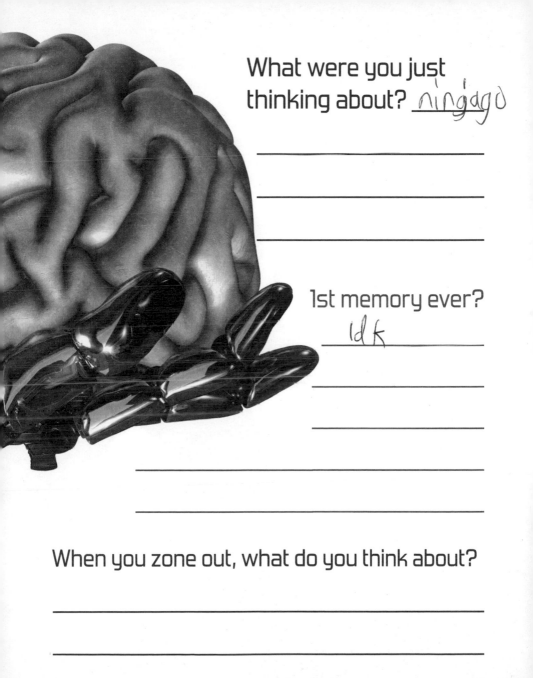

What were you just
thinking about? _ninjago_

_____

_____

_____

1st memory ever?

_Idk_____

_____

_____

_____

_____

When you zone out, what do you think about?

_____

_____

Would you rather have the power to control

o Fire o Water

o Air d Earth?

Why? What would you do with your power?

Kill people

# YOU ARE THE PROUD OWNER OF A HLY LARGE RAT.

*oh yeah!*

**pros**                    **cons**

_____     _____

_____     _____

_____     _____

_____     _____

_____     _____

_____     _____

# WHAT DO YOU THINK OF WHEN YOU SEE THESE WORDS?

Write down the first thing that comes to your incredibly mega mind. It can be another word, sentence, or super short story.

**wart** _shoop da woop_

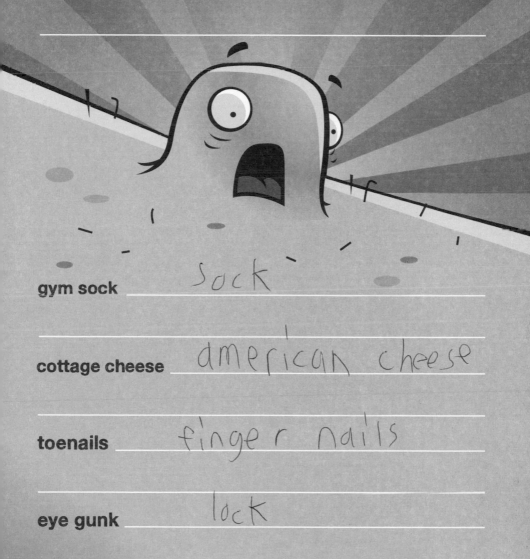

**gym sock** _sock_

**cottage cheese** _american cheese_

**toenails** _finger nails_

**eye gunk** _lock_

# Describe the last really bizzaro dREAM you had.

_____

_____

_____

_____

_____

_____

_____

**1.** ☑ Zombie
☐ Ghost
☐ Monster movie?

2. Last piece of food you spit out? _ _ _ _ _ _ _ _ _ _ _ _

3. Who deserves a pie in the face? _ _ _ _ _ _ _ _ _ _ _

4. Your shoes smell? ☐ Yep, they're pretty ripe.
   ☑ Nope, fresh as a mountain breeze.

5. Last girl you talked to? ~~_____~~ nevermind. _ _ _ _ _ _

6. If you could name a newly discovered planet, what would you call it? _ _ _ _ fart zone _ _ _ _ _ _ _ _ _ _

7. Your best pool move? ☐ Dive ☐ Belly flop ☐ Cannon ball

8. Think SpongeBob will ever get his license? ☐ Sure ☑ Nah

9. Is ☐ Squidward a jerk ☑ SpongeBob annoying ☐ Both?

10. Ever feed a sibling a non-food item? ☐ No

   ☐ Yes, gave _ _ _ _ _ _ _ _ a _ _ _ _ _ _ _ _ _ _.

# INKBLOT TEST

Describe what you see in the
inkblot.

Then flip book
upside down.

_____

_____

_____

_____

_____

# MISSION TO THE MOO

You've been chosen to set up a colony
with a race of space aliens on the moon.
You can take 2 friends, 2 food items to share,
& some games. Who & what would u take & why?

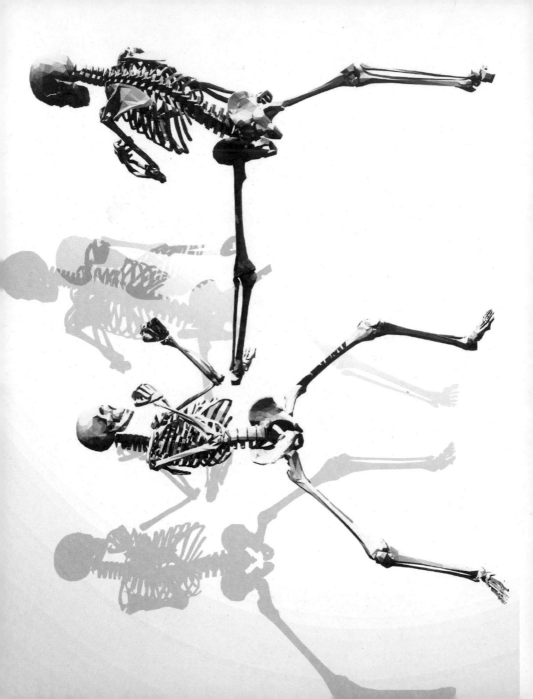

# Whoa DUDE! That Hurt!

Keep a file of all your injuries - cuts, bruises, or busted butt (from attempting to kickbox your bro).

Injury

How'd it happen?

# HUMAN EXPERIMENT

## #1

**What's the #1 thing you like to do?**

computor

**Now, try to go 1 week without doing it.**

 **Report what happens.**

I aready did.

# YOU'RE THE PRESIDENT OF THE U. S. OF A. WHAT SPECIAL ROOMS AND OUTSIDE AREAS WOULD YOU ADD TO THE WHITE HOUSE?

lego stadium

# THE STARE-OFF

# HiDDEN TALENTS

Grab a friend. Hold a staring contest.

Who won? {       }

Now ask your friend to time how long
you can hold your breath. {       }

your time

Now time him 👉 {       }

his time

Ok, now thumb wrestle your bud.

Who won? {       }

Now, the spitting contest.

And the winner is ... {       }

Finally, the burping contest. You might
need a 3rd party to judge this one.

Best BELCHER is 👉 {       }

**1.** What one question would you ask an alien?

you're fat, arent you?

ASH

DUDE

2. Best fair food?

☑ Funnel cakes ☐ Italian sausages ☐ Fried anything

3. Would you wear panty hose over your head for $5?

☑ No ☐ Sure, why not?

4. Last thing you threw up? _ _ _ _ _ _ _ _ _ _ _ _ _ _ _

5. Ever been lost? ☐ Nope ☑ Yep, I ⌂ _ sched _ _ _ _ _ _ .

6. Coldest you've ever been? _ _ _ _ _ _ _ _ _ _ _ _

7. Hottest you've ever been? _ _ _ _ _ _ _ _ _ _ _ _

8. Eat things you drop on the ground?

☑ No ☐ Sure, 3-second rule man.

9. Have any scabs? ☐ No ☐ Yes, from _ _ _ _ _ _ _ _ _ .

10. Something you keep hidden? _ this book _ _ _ _ _

# YOU OWN A MAGIC ROCK THAT CAN BECOME WHATEVER YOU WISH FOR. WHAT WOULD YOU WANT IT TO CHANGE INTO? WHY?

ultimate Lego world

DRAW OR DESCRIBE YOUR LATEST CRISIS FOR THE HEROES TO SOLVE. YOU KNOW, A FIGHT WITH A FRIEND, IN TROUBLE WITH PARENTS, OR YOUR ESCAPED PET IGUANA.

# People say a lot of STUFF!

Certain words, sayings, or maybe it's something they're always telling you to do. Fill in names of friends, family, etc. and what they say.

name

name

name

name

# RAGEOUS
## TS,

funny stories, and stuff that's so gross it's hysterical. Keep all the deets right here.

# HUMAN EXPERIMENT

## #2

Come up with a new name for yourself.
(A nickname, something funny, or just one
you've always liked.) Try to convince everyone
to call you by your new name.

Document what happens.

Dude,
that's
serious!

$tuPID

Jeffry

I told you.
My name is
Catfish!

# WHAT ANNOYING THINGS DO YOUR FRIENDS OR BROS AND SISTERS DO? {LIKE A LITTLE SISTER PLAYING DRESS-UP WITH YOUR DOG SPIKE}

I can't stand it when _____

_____

_____

_____

_____

_____

_____

_____

_____

_____

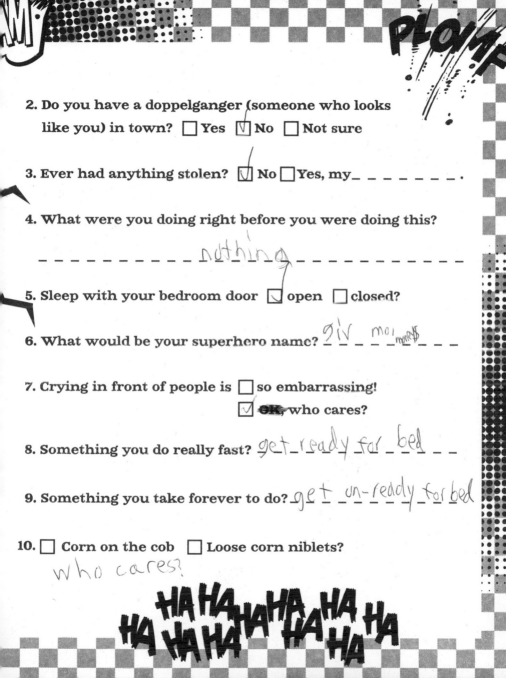

2. Do you have a doppelganger (someone who looks like you) in town? ☐ Yes ☑ No ☐ Not sure

3. Ever had anything stolen? ☑ No ☐ Yes, my_ _ _ _ _ _ _ .

4. What were you doing right before you were doing this?
_ _ _ _ _ _ _ _ _ nothing _ _ _ _ _ _ _

5. Sleep with your bedroom door ☑ open ☐ closed?

6. What would be your superhero name? giv_ moi money_ _

7. Crying in front of people is ☐ so embarrassing!
☑ ~~OK,~~ who cares?

8. Something you do really fast? get ready for bed _ _

9. Something you take forever to do? get un-ready for bed

10. ☐ Corn on the cob ☐ Loose corn niblets?
who cares?

HA HA HA HA HA HA HA HA HA HA HA HA HA

# PARALLEL UNIVERSES

You get to live 2 completely different lives at the same time.
Describe them — where you live, what you do, family, friends, etc.

**LiFE 1** _ben_

**LiFE 2** _pilot_

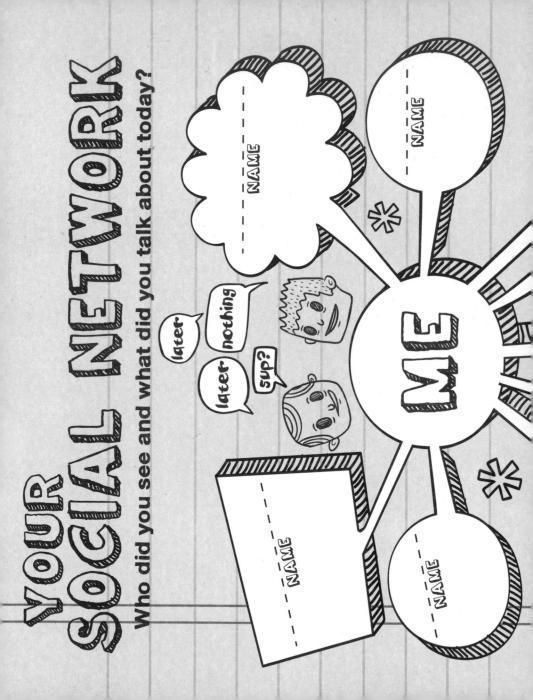

HERE IS YOUR
VERY OWN
BLACK HOLE

# LIST OR DRAW STUFF YOU'D LIKE TO SEND INTO IT.

STAY AWAY
FROM IT, MAN!

{ **Black hole**
*noun*
a region of space having a gravitational
field so intense that no matter or radiation
can escape }

Get some paint
& leave
your personal
graffiti on this page.

It's totally legal.

DESCRIBE ALL
THE DETAILS
OF YOUR DAY.
WRITE EVERY-
THING
BACKWARDS.

Hold this up        to a mirror.

No way, dude.
you oh! no way

~~you oh! no way~~

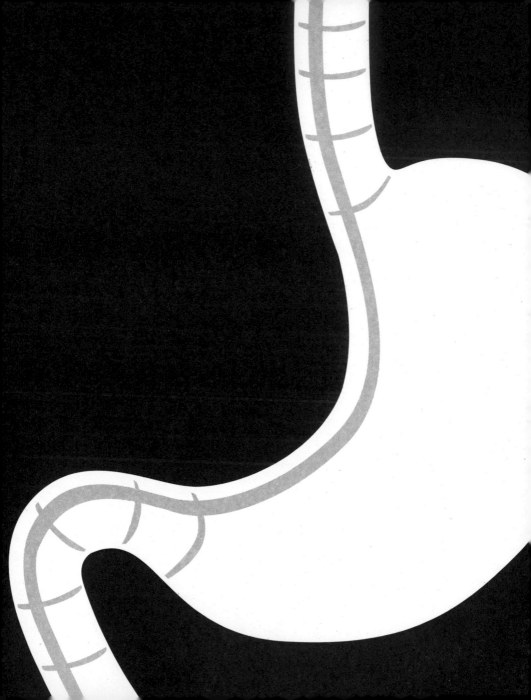

# WHAT DID YOU PUT IN YOUR GUT  TODAY?

_____

_____

_____

_____

_____

_____

 _____

# NOW, DRAW ALL OF IT IN ORDER OF HOW IT ENTERED!

# GAME

KEEP A LOG OF ALL THE AMAZING **SPORTS** PLAYS
OR MOVES YOU SEE OR DO.
(OR, ANY AMAZING **GAMING** FEATS.)

# ON!

## THE UNFAIR CALL, COACH PLAYING FAVES, OR THE UNSPORTSMANLIKE SPORTSMAN. KEEP TRACK.

# THE ULTIMATE SANDWICH

List everything you can think of to put in a sandwich.
Ask around if you run out of ideas.
Then draw your creation.

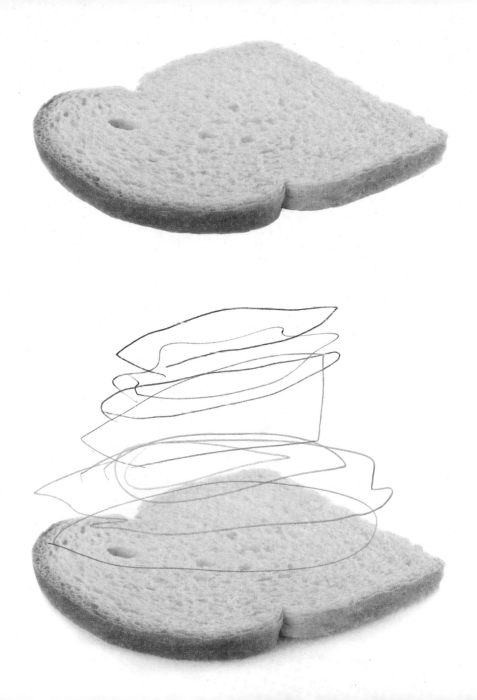

2. ☑ **Karate chopping Styrofoam**

   ☐ **Popping Bubble Wrap is more fun.**

3. **Air** ☑ **drums** ☐ **guitar?**

4. **Last game you lost?** _ _ _ _ _ _ _ _ _ _ _ _ _ _

5. **Last game you won?** _ _ _ _ _ _ _ _ _ _ _ _ _ _

6. **Buffets are** ☐ **so awesome** ☐ **OK** ☐ **kinda gross.**

7. **Ever shake or kick a vending machine?**
   ☑ **Yes** ☐ **No, it could crush you!**

8. **Best thing to slurp through a straw?** chclate _ milk_

9. **Is your 2nd toe longer than your big one?** ☐ **Yep** ☑ **Nope**

10. **Sneakiest place you've ever hidden?** berind _ a_
    door

CRASH!

☞ **6:29 a.m.** . . . . . this . . . . . . . . . . . . . . . . . . . . .

. . . . . . . . . . . . . . . . . . . . . . . . . . . . . . . . .

. . . . . . . . . . . . . . . . . . . . . . . . . . . . . . . . .

☞ **9:12 a.m.** . . . . . this . . . . . . . . . . . . . . . . . . . . .

. . . . . . . . . . . . . . . . . . . . . . . . . . . . . . . . .

. . . . . . . . . . . . . . . . . . . . . . . . . . . . . . . . .

☞ **12:17 p.m.** . . . . . this . . . . . . . . . . . . . . . . . . . . .

. . . . . . . . . . . . . . . . . . . . . . . . . . . . . . . . .

. . . . . . . . . . . . . . . . . . . . . . . . . . . . . . . . .

☞ **2:23 p.m.** . . . . this . . . . . . . . . . . . . . . . . . . . .

. . . . . . . . . . . . . . . . . . . . . . . . . . . . . . . . .

. . . . . . . . . . . . . . . . . . . . . . . . . . . . . . . . .

☞ **5:59 p.m.** . . . . this . . . . . . . . . . . . . . . . . . . . .

. . . . . . . . . . . . . . . . . . . . . . . . . . . . . . . . .

. . . . . . . . . . . . . . . . . . . . . . . . . . . . . . . . .

☞ **10:43 p.m.** . . . . . this . . . . . . . . . . . . . . . . . . . . .

. . . . . . . . . . . . . . . . . . . . . . . . . . . . . . . . .

. . . . . . . . . . . . . . . . . . . . . . . . . . . . . . . . .

# I DESERVE AN AWARD FOR...

WRITE WHATEVER YOU'RE TOTALLY AWESOME AT ON THIS TROPHY.
BEST ARM FARTER EVER, FASTEST TEXTER, CHORE SHIRKER, OR GUITAR HERO.
LIST OTHER STUFF YOU ROCK AT!

LEGO MASTER

# You are gonna be a HUGE star.
# Get Ready.

You will need a bio and a picture to go along with it. So draw a picture of your famous self with your dog, cat, pet rat, whatever.

Now come up with a famous bio. Include what you're famous for — like inventing the first robot with feelings — plus your hobbies, where you live, and so on.

_____

_____

_____

_____

_____

_____

Write something that creeps you out in the big
bubble. Then, think of 3 other things that word
makes you think of and write those words in the
connecting bubbles. Keep moving thru all the
bubbles until they are filled.
It's your

# MIND MAP.

_____
is creepy.
It makes
me think
of

which makes
me think of

which makes
me think of

BEST BRAIN EVER

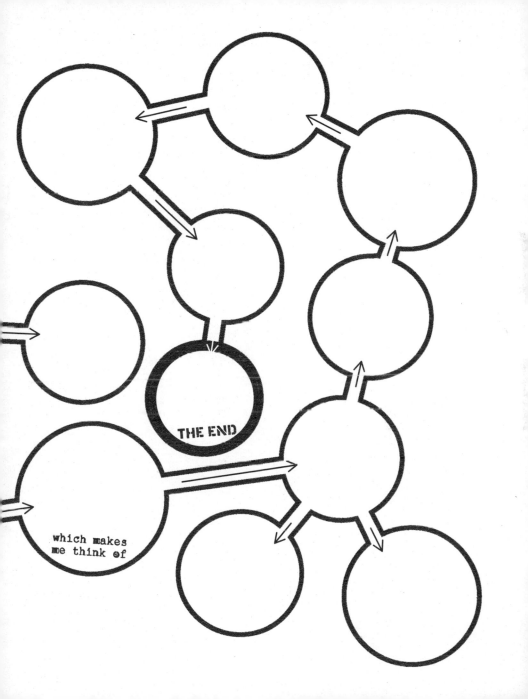

# List anything that

army of
vampires,
giant
screeching
animal

# What's your least favorite school lunch? Why?

**Now draw it.** 👉

slime

# LEAVE YOUR MARK!

BOOOMM!!

**COMBINE A WORD FROM THIS LIST**

**WITH ANOTHER WORD FROM THIS LIST**

CAPTAIN
COMMANDER
MISTER
CHEF
KING
LIEUTENANT
VICEROY
CHIEF

LOOGIE
TOE JAM
HAIR BALL
LABRADOODLE
GAS BEGONE
DUNG BEETLE
HAIR LICE
EARWAX

**PUT YOUR WORD COMBO HERE.**

LEAVE YOUR WORD COMBO WHEREVER YOU GO THIS WEEK. CHALK IT ON A SIDEWALK, DRAW IT IN THE DIRT, SIGN STUFF WITH IT.

SO, HOW DID PEOPLE REACT TO IT? _____

_____

How many teeth do you have?

1. ☐

**2. Can you touch your tongue to your nose?** ☐ yep ☑ nope

**3. Best food served on a stick?** _ _ _ _ _ _ _ _ _ _ _ _ _ _ _

**4. Are you more of a** ☑ sneakers ☐ flip-flops **kind of guy?**

**5. Rather have giant** ☑ lobster claws for hands
☐ lizard tail on your butt?

**6. Which reeks worse?** ☐ Your armpits ☑ Your feet

**7.** ☐ Slice of pie ☐ Fried pie?

**8. What combo makes the nastiest smoothie?**

_ _ _ _ _ _ _ _ _ _ _ _ & _ _ _ _ _ _ _ _ _ _ _ _

**9. Afraid of roaches?** ☐ No way, man.
☑ Yeah, they're totally gross.

**10. Do you have toe jam?** ☐ Yes ☑ No ☐ What's that?

# Would you rather have

**1 enormous**

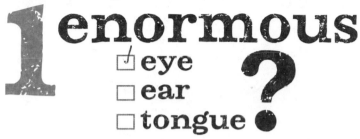

- ☑ eye
- ☐ ear
- ☐ tongue

**?**

## What cool things could you do?

see thru

# KEEP ALL YOUR FAVORITE  LINES FROM MOVIES, TV SHOWS, & CARTOONS HERE.

DUDES LIKE TO USE THEM WHEN THEY TALK TO EACH OTHER.

bill cosby himself

{ why did you do that? }
Name of movie, show, cartoon

i dont know.

{ _ _ _ _ _ _ _ _ _ _ _ _ _ }
Name of movie, show, cartoon

{ _ _ _ _ _ _ _ _ _ _ _ _ _ }
Name of movie, show, cartoon

{ _ _ _ _ _ _ _ _ _ _ _ _ _ }
Name of movie, show, cartoon

{ _ _ _ _ _ _ _ _ _ _ _ _ _ }
Name of movie, show, cartoon

SAVE THE ROACHES!

OUTLAW STINKY PERFUME!

MORE FRIES!

# ORGANIZE YOUR OWN PROTEST.
## (WELL, ON PAPER AT LEAST.)

**Make a list of world, home, school, etc.
changes you'd like to make.**

_____    _____

_____    _____

_____    _____

_____    _____

_____    _____

_____    _____

_____    _____

_____    _____

 **Then make a sign for the most important one.**

# HERE IS YOUR VIRTUAL TIME CAPSULE.

It's one of those things a lot of schools fill up with stuff that's important to current society and then bury. Then a teacher says, "People will uncover this 100 - 200 years from now and study it."
Well here's your chance to make a way cooler one full of stuff all about YOU.
Draw, list, or tape down stuff you'd want future people to know about you.
Photo, piece of your fave gum, etc. YEAH!

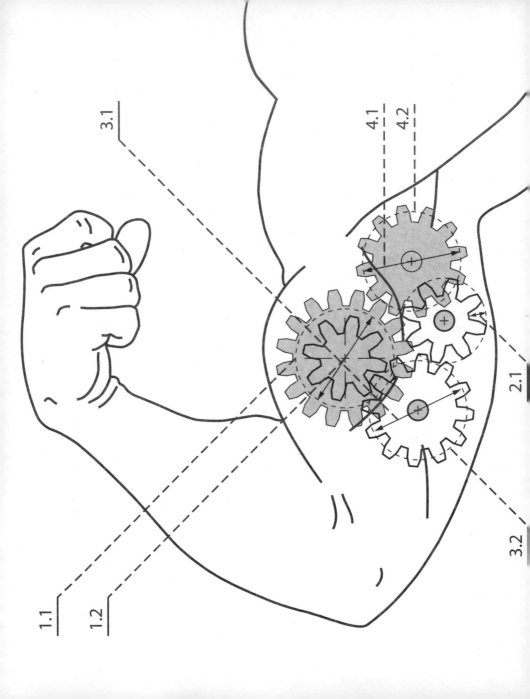

# ARM YOURSELF WITH KNOWLEDGE

Find out what teachers, coaches, family, friends, and even bullies are really into. You never know when you'll need this information — like when you need to give your teacher a gift because you're the less-than-perfect kid.

| NAME | STUFF THEY LIKE | NAME | STUFF THEY LIKE |
|------|-----------------|------|-----------------|
|      |                 |      |                 |
|      |                 |      |                 |
|      |                 |      |                 |
|      |                 |      |                 |

Which is grosser? Green ☐ mold ☑ mucus

Who's cooler? Green ☑ Lantern ☐ Arrow

☐ Leafy green spinach ☑ Broccoli is the worst!

I ☐ believe ☑ don't believe in little green men.

☐ Real ☐ Goofy golf?

Would u try green eggs & ham? ☑ rep ☐ No way!

Green ☐ slime ☐ goo ☑ algae is the nastiest!

3 wishes you would ask from a
   crazy little leprechaun?

   1. _____

   2. _____

   3. _____

# If you could be any sort of WILD ANIMAL, what would you be & why?

_____

_____

_____

_____

_____

_____

_____

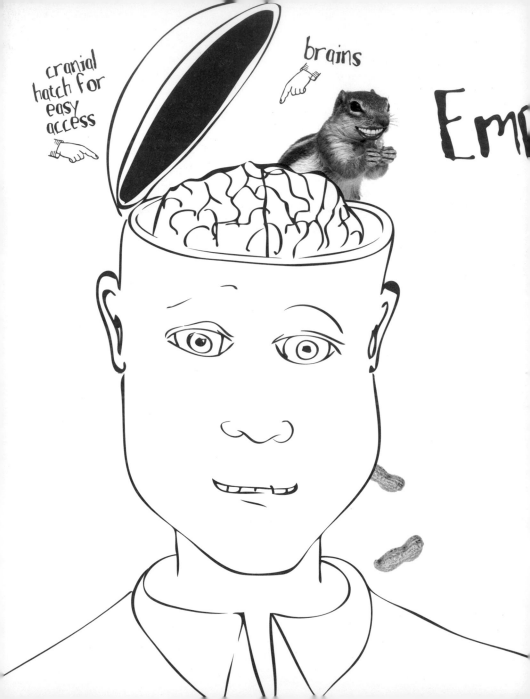

y all your brain stuff **HERE** 👉

Laugh-out-loud jokes, random THOUGHTS, crazy inventions, WEIRD dreams, pranks you're planning. Write, Draw, DESTROY!

WRITE HERE

WRITE HERE

whatev's

WRITE HERE

WRITE HERE

Dude!
Foul!

WRITE HERE

BRRAAAP!

WRITE HERE

WRITE HERE

WRITE HERE

What's he thinkin', dude?

What's he sayin', dude?

WRITE HERE

WRITE HERE

Bro, if you think this book is totally sweet, then check out the original world of write, draw, destroy — DUDE & DUDE ~~DIARY~~. And if that's not enough, go to

# www.thedudebook.com

for even more totally random stuff!